Napkin Folding

Elegant Yet Easy Ideas to Transform Your Table

By Dominique De Vito

Cider Mill Press
Kennebunkport, Maine

Cider Mill Press Book Publishers
"Where good books are ready for press"
12 Port Farm Road
Kennebunkport, Maine 04046

Visit us on the Web!
www.cidermillpress.com

Design by Alicia Freile, Tango Media
Typeset by Gwen Galeone, Tango Media
Typography: Dorchester Script MT, MrsEaves, and P22 Garamouche Ornaments
All illustrations courtesy of Sherry Berger
Cover photo courtesy of Getty Images
Printed in China

1 2 3 4 5 6 7 8 9 0
First Edition

Contents

Introduction

It wasn't too long ago that every member of the family had his or her own napkin that was to be used for every meal over the course of a week or so, until it was washed and then put back on the table for reuse.

In order to make a gathering seem festive or special, the simple napkin assigned to each place setting needed to be elaborated upon. Starting with a clean, starched linen and folding it into decorative and fanciful shapes was an easy way to do this.

Even today, when the paper napkin still rules the weekday family table and is considered acceptable for some dinner parties, folding the napkin this way and that to create an elegant or whimsical shape turns a routine gathering into a special one. Adults appreciate the change of pace, and kids enjoy the designs — and love recreating them or trying new ones.

The great thing about playing with napkins to create fun shapes is that it can be as simple or elaborate as you like. You may decide that your Sunday dinners should be the occasions where you set a more formal table by including a special fold. Or you may challenge the kids to come up with fun folds that make setting the table more enjoyable for them.

This book gives you step-by-step instructions for creating 50 folds that range from extremely easy to fairly complicated. The napkin that's included with the book is the perfect size for practicing the folds, so you'll soon get the hang of it. As you gather round the table you've set with fancifully folded napkins, take pleasure in the presentation — and be thankful you don't have to use the same napkin all week!

A WELL-SET TABLE

How strictly you follow table setting "rules" depends on your personality as the host. You can be as formal as you wish. Alternately, you can consider these rules simply as guidelines and work around them as your creative flair dictates. It's truly up to you.

❖ When setting the table, you should leave approximately 18 inches for each place setting, if you can. You don't want them to look crowded. The bottom tip of the plate, as well as the bottoms of the silverware, should line up two inches from the edge of the table.

❖ Arrange your silverware in order of use, starting at the outside and working toward the plate. Only put out utensils that will be used during the meal, placing one utensil per course. Forks go to the left of the plate, and knives and spoons go to the right (with knives placed next to the plate, their edges pointing toward the plate, followed by the spoons). An exception to this is the seafood fork, which goes on the right, next to the spoons.

❖ Place the glassware to the right of the plate, above the tip of the dinner knife. These are also placed in order of use, with the water glass closest to the plate. Wine glasses follow to the right.

❖ Bring tea and coffee cups in when it is time to serve. You can do the same for dessert plates and silverware, especially if you need to conserve space.

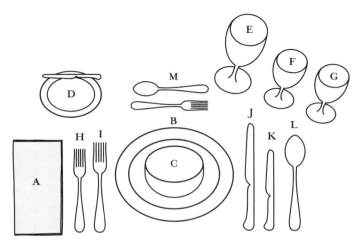

A Formal Place Setting

A. Napkin (with folds facing the forks); B. Dinner plate; C. Soup bowl; D. Bread plate and butter knife; E. Water glass; F. Red wine glass; G. White wine glass; H. Salad fork; I. Dinner fork; J. Dinner knife; K. Salad knife, L. Soup spoon, M. Dessert fork and spoon (optional)

A Less Formal Setting

If you're not serving a first course, place the napkin at the center of the plate and place the salad plate to the left of the forks. Set a teaspoon next to the knife for dessert.

A. Dinner plate; B. Salad plate; C. Bread plate; D. Water glass; E. Fork; F. Knife; G. Dessert spoon; H. Napkin

Napkin Placement

Traditionally, the napkin is folded into a rectangle and placed to the left of the forks, with the folds toward the plate. If there isn't enough room for this, the napkin is sometimes placed under the forks.

Of course, the whole purpose of this book is to make the napkin the focal point of the place setting, and you'll be placing your napkins on the plate, above the plate, below the plate, in a glass, and more! Below are some placement suggestions for the types of folds included in this book.

To the Left

Try any of your smaller folds here. The Traditional Dinner and Luncheon folds (page 14 and 15) look great here, as do the Ascot (page 16) and the Together Forever (page 46). Large folds demand more attention and will look better in the center of the plate or in a glass.

To the Right

Your upright folds will look nice next to the glasses (above the spoons). Try the Pope's Bonnet (page 21), Pine Cone (page 32), and Paper Vase (page 39) in this location.

Above the Plate

Folds with strong silhouettes will look good here, such as the Classic Fan (page 28), Invitation (page 54), and Double Fan (page 60).

In the Center

Full folds and others you simply *must* show off belong in the center. You can also place in the center a glass with the folded napkin in it. Try the Monogram Show-Off (page 18), Inner Tube (page 24), Fleur-de-Lis (page 38), and others in this position.

Below the Plate

Try this napkin position when you'd like an unusual look. Rolled napkins look good here, such as the Banded Beauty (page 31) and the Candle (page 36).

In a Glass

For a festive look that will delight your guests, use a fold that is placed inside a glass. You can keep the glass in its conventional location or move it to the center of the plate. The Rainbow (page 20) and the Blossom (page 41) are just two examples of folds to place inside a glass.

STAIN REMOVAL

No matter how pretty, formal, or decorative your napkins are, and no matter the formal rules (which dictate that napkins are intended only for removing crumbs from the mouth), stains happen.

Now, all stain experts agree: The secret of removing stains is to treat them immediately. In fact, the longer a stain sets, the harder it is to remove. What most stain experts don't realize, however, is that it may be hours before you can collect and clean the linens. My advice is to get to the linens as soon as you can, but don't let it ruin your affair.

After your meal, collect the napkins, and soak them in a clean sink or pail filled with ice-cold water. If you're too tired to do the laundry right away, leave them in the water overnight. When you're ready, drain the water, spray any light stains with a commercial spray stain treatment, and launder. (When choosing a laundry detergent, find one that contains enzymes or "protein stain remover.") Avoid the dryer, and let them dry in the sunlight.

Some stubborn stains may require extra care. Following are tips for dealing with the most common culprits that will threaten your linens.

Wine

For a fresh red-wine stain, sponge white vinegar onto the spot while it's still wet, and then let the napkin soak in cold water until you launder it. If the stain has dried, soak in a heavy-duty detergent solution (½ teaspoon enzyme-containing detergent and ½ cup warm water), and then launder in warm water.

For white wine, let the stain soak in an ammonia solution (1 tablespoon ammonia to 1 cup water). If the stain has dried, soak in cold water, and then launder in warm water.

Try to avoid mopping up a wine spill on your tablecloth with your napkin, because then you'll have two pieces to clean up. Instead, slide a small towel under the spill, dab it with a cold, wet cloth, and then sprinkle salt over the stain to keep it from spreading.

Fruit and Fruit Juices

Sprinkle the stain with salt to soak up the liquid. Spray with a solution of two-thirds water to one-third white vinegar, and then launder. For a tough stain, dip the napkin repeatedly in boiling water, and then dab it with lemon juice before laundering.

Tea

For fresh tea stains, rinse the stain under cold water, soak, and then launder. If the stain has dried, drape the napkin over a bowl. Sprinkle with Borax laundry detergent until the stain is covered. Then pour boiling water around the stain, working toward the center. Repeat if necessary.

Coffee

Rinse in warm water, and then soak in a solution of ½ teaspoon detergent and ½ cup warm water, or in a Borax solution (2 cups of water to 1 tablespoon Borax).

Chocolate

Sponge the stain with liquid dish detergent, and then launder. If the stain is stubborn, follow the directions for dried tea stain.

Gravy

Soak the stain in cold water. (Warm water will set the stain.) Then sponge diluted laundry detergent onto the spot before laundering.

Oil, Fat, and Grease

Dab the stain gently with a paper towel to blot any excess grease, and then launder. For best results, you can also pre-wash the spot in warm, sudsy water before laundering.

Eggs

Sponge with cold, salty water. Rinse when the stain has disappeared, and then soak in a solution a solution of ½ teaspoon detergent to ½ cup warm water.

Ketchup and Tomato Sauce

Hold the stain under cold running water, and rub between your fingers. Apply an enzyme pre-wash treatment, and then launder.

Mustard

Rub the stain between your fingers in a mild detergent solution, and then sponge with an ammonia solution (1 tablespoon ammonia and 1 cup of water).

Lipstick

Rub the stain with rubbing alcohol or a lukewarm laundry-detergent solution (½ teaspoon detergent and ½ cup warm water).

Candle Wax

Let the wax harden completely before removing it from your linen with a butter knife. Then place paper towels under and over the napkin, and rub a warm iron over one side. Flip and repeat. Change the towels often, as they will be absorbing the wax. Treat any color marks with rubbing alcohol — or make it a rule to only use white candles!

Gum

Harden the gum with an ice cube, or put the napkin in the freezer. Then scrape the gum off with a blunt knife.

Mildew

Launder and then let the napkin dry in the sunlight.

Traditional Dinner Fold

You can't go wrong with this fold. Some even like to iron their linen napkins into this fold and store them that way so that when it is time to use them, they are ready to go and look great. This napkin can be placed to the left of the forks, underneath the dinner fork, or in the middle of the plate.

INSTRUCTIONS:

1. Using a square napkin, position it in front of you so that the flat sides face up and down.

2. Fold the top half down to form a rectangle.

3. Working from the left, fold the napkin in so that it forms a square.

4. Repeat this fold to create a rectangular fold.

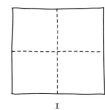

1

3

4

Traditional Luncheon Fold

Like its rectangular affiliate, the triangular fold makes an easy and elegant statement that, while slightly less formal, is always appropriate and always simple to accomplish. This napkin is best placed to the left of or underneath the dinner fork.

INSTRUCTIONS:

1. Using a square napkin, position it in front of you so that the flat sides face up and down.

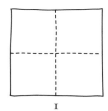

I

2. Fold the top half down to form a rectangle.

3. Working from the left, fold the napkin in so that it forms a square.

3

4. Working from the bottom right corner, fold the napkin up to form a triangle with the corner facing left.

4

Ascot

In five easy moves, you can create a napkin that goes from being ordinary to elegant — especially if you're working with linen that has a monogram. The effect is equally striking with a large, colorful napkin. The best places to position this fold are to the left of the fork or in the center of the plate.

INSTRUCTIONS:

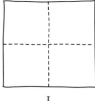

1

3

4

5

1. Fold the napkin in half and then in half again so it is quartered. (If you're working with a paper napkin, it is probably already quartered; just unfold it to be sure.)

2. Position the napkin so that it is in a diamond rather than square orientation.

3. Fold the top pointed corner down.

4. Bring in the pointed corners on the left, and then the right, so they meet in the middle.

5. Press down to crease the edges, and turn the napkin over.

Extra Ascot

If you like the look of the Ascot, you can add a couple more folds to create another layer to the napkin. As with the Ascot, if you're using a monogrammed napkin, this is a great way to showcase the embroidery. If not, it is still a great fold, and you can position it up or down! When faced up, this fold can be tucked into a napkin ring as well.

INSTRUCTIONS:

1. Fold the napkin in half, and then in half again so it is quartered.

2. Position the napkin so that it is in a diamond rather than square orientation.

3. Fold the top pointed corner down, and then turn the napkin over.

4. Bring in the pointed corners on the left, and then the right, so they meet in the middle.

5. Press down to crease the edges, and turn the napkin over.

1

3

4

5

Monogram Show-Off

This is the fanciest of the folds that show off your monogrammed linens. If you've mastered the Ascot and the Extra Ascot, you'll enjoy playing with this one to get it right. And you'll enjoy how nicely it shows off your initials! Put this one in the center of the dinner plate.

INSTRUCTIONS:

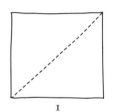

1. Fold the napkin in half to form a triangle, being sure to position your monogram on the underside and on the center point.

2. Working with the point facing down, bring the point that's facing right in and across the napkin so it passes over the other side. Firmly crease the fold.

3. Next, bring the point back and over, forming a crease in the center of the napkin.

4. Complete the right-hand part of the fold by bringing in the point again and folding it so it goes toward the bottom.

5. Repeat steps 2–4, but with the point on the left.

6. Turn the napkin over.

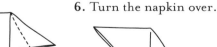

Tied to Perfection

When your get-together is casual, but you want
to do something a little different, this is the fold
to bring your table together. It won't work with
paper, either, so a linen napkin takes it from being
a bit crude to definitely dashing.

INSTRUCTIONS:

1. Fold a large,
   square napkin in half diagonally to
   form a triangle.

2. Place the point of the triangle facing
   down, so the flat surface is on the top.

3. From the bottom, begin rolling up
   the napkin, and continue until it's
   all rolled up.

4. Tie the rolled napkin in a knot.

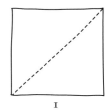

I

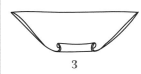

3

4

Rainbow

Place settings can be accentuated with napkins that adorn water and wine glasses, too. These kinds of folds typically extend straight up or fold over to give a more or less formal look to the table. This fold complements a short water glass or tall wine glass — or it can be threaded through a napkin ring to achieve a similar effect lying down on a plate.

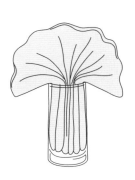

INSTRUCTIONS:

1. Using a square napkin, fold it from top to bottom to form a rectangle.

2. Working from the right or left side, begin making accordion pleats of approximately one inch.

3. Hold the bottom of the napkin until it is placed inside the glass or through the napkin ring. The bottom should stay tightly folded while the top loosens into a rainbow shape.

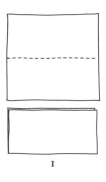

1

2

Pope's Bonnet

It's amazing how much this folded napkin, which stands on its own, looks like the Pope's hat or a fancy crown of some sort. Using colored napkins can make this one stand out even more, and giving it center stage on the plate helps, too.

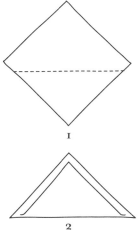
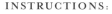

I

2

INSTRUCTIONS:

1. Fold a square napkin in half so that it forms a triangle.

2. With the point facing down, bring in the points from the left and the right so the bottom edges align, but so there is about an inch of space between them.

3. Bring the top of the napkin down until it is an inch or so from the bottom corner.

4. Fold back the top inch or so of this fold, leaving an inch or so between its edge and what is now the bottom edge.

5. Turn the napkin over, and then hold it so that it is almost standing. Bring the right and left edges in toward each other, and interlock them to form a tube.

6. Stand the napkin up with the folded side facing forward.

4

5

6

Triple Fold

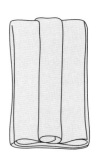

If you want a fold that's going to give you clean lines to help accentuate the pattern of your china, consider this one. Placed in the center of the plate, it gives the impression of paper waiting to be written upon or a conversation about to unfold.

I

2

3

INSTRUCTIONS:

1. Working from the top of a square napkin, begin folding it into quarters lengthwise, folding one quarter over the other so that it's almost a roll.

2. With the folded edge at the bottom, lift the last layer of the cloth and roll it cigarette-style into the middle of the napkin.

3. Fold the napkin in half so that the center fold is front-and-center.

Ripples

This is a softer version of the Triple Fold just described. It is especially nice with a patterned linen or a paper napkin.

INSTRUCTIONS:

1. Starting with a square napkin, fold it in thirds to form a thin rectangle.

2. With the folded edge on top, bring the right-hand edge over, and fold it so that it is about two inches long.

3. Repeat Step 2.

4. Repeat Steps 2 and 3 with the left side of the napkin.

5. Now fold the right side of the napkin under the left side, exposing three folded edges on the right side. Separate the folds slightly as you position the napkin on the table.

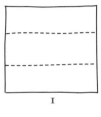

I

2

3

4

5

Inner Tube

This is a great fold to use when you want to decorate a simple napkin with a belt motif. The "belt" can be anything from a handsome, thick silver napkin ring to a paper loop decorated to look like a Pilgrim's belt-buckle. The napkin becomes almost secondary to the look and feel of whatever is keeping it rolled up.

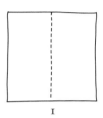

1

2

INSTRUCTIONS:

1. Fold a square napkin in half to form a rectangle.

2. Working from the bottom, roll the napkin up like you'd roll up a sleeping bag.

3. Secure it with a napkin ring or "belt" of some sort.

Extended Crescent

This makes for a great napkin to put in a glass at the breakfast table, as sleepyheads or latecomers to the table might find the food in front of them before they've had a chance to get their napkin. Hopefully they won't pour juice on it!

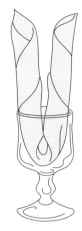

INSTRUCTIONS:

1. Positioning a square napkin so it is in a diamond shape, start rolling up from the bottom point.

2. When the napkin is completely rolled up, it will look like a crescent roll.

3. Fold it in the middle so the last tip of the roll is in the center, and then place it in the glass.

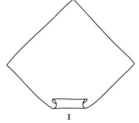

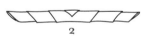

I

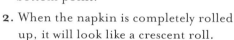

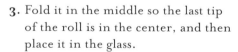

2

3

Sphinx

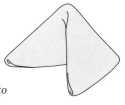

When folded with the two tips facing forward, this one is reminiscent of the paws of the Sphinx of ancient Egypt. Fortunately, it takes far less time to create than one of the wonders of the ancient world.

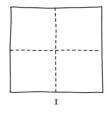

I

2

3

INSTRUCTIONS:

1. Fold a large, square napkin into quarters, placing the loose corners in the upper right.

2. Fold the bottom-left corner toward the top-right corner.

3. Lift in the center so that the napkin stands.

Server Serviette

The word for napkin in French is **serviette.**
Here's a beautiful way to use a napkin to hold
silverware rather than frame it.

INSTRUCTIONS:

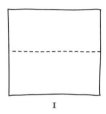

1

2

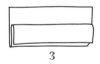

3

4

5

1. Fold a large,
   square napkin in half horizontally to
   form a rectangle.

2. With the folded edge at the bottom,
   fold back the first layer so that it is
   folded in half toward the bottom edge.

3. Turn the napkin over, and fold the left
   edge over until it reaches the center.

4. Roll this part over two more times so
   that it forms a secure pocket.

5. Position the napkin with the loose
   fold in back, and fill with a fork, knife,
   and spoon.

Classic Fan

This fold looks great placed either in the center of the plate or just above it. It is easy and fun to create, and it never fails to impress.

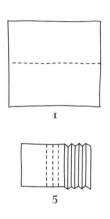

1

5

6

INSTRUCTIONS:

1. Start with the napkin in its open square configuration.

2. Fold it in half to form a rectangle.

3. Starting at one end, fold the edge over about an inch, pressing to create a firm crease.

4. Fold this over again so there is a double fold. This will create a solid base.

5. Next, create accordion pleats of the same size as your original fold. Continue about halfway down the napkin. Firmly crease the pleats.

6. With the half of the napkin that remains, fold up from the bottom-left, tucking the end into the pleats.

7. Stand the napkin up so that the pleats fall into place.

Fan-Dango

The fandango is actually a folk dance dating to 16th-century Portugal. Impress your guests with this bit of trivia while they marvel at the festive napkin on their plate! Like the Inner Tube, this fold comes to life depending on what you use to secure it in the middle.

I

2

3

INSTRUCTIONS:

1. Working with a large, square napkin, fold the top down and the bottom up so their edges meet in the center.

2. Starting on the left or right side, create an accordion pleat along the narrow length of the napkin.

3. Once the napkin ring or other decorative holder is in the middle, fan out the sides to bring it to its full beauty.

All Aboard

When you're in the mood to set sail, this cute fold that resembles a sailboat of sorts can be the flagship of your table, which you can accent with other items to set a nautical theme. Use a large napkin for this one (a 17- to 20-inch cloth).

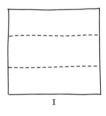

I

2

3

4

5

INSTRUCTIONS:

1. Working with a large square, fold the napkin in thirds so that it forms a rectangle.

2. Place the folded edge on top, and with your finger in the center, fold the right side down so that the edge is along the center.

3. Repeat Step 2 with the left side of the napkin.

4. Next, fold the bottom edges up so they are even with the edge on the bottom layer.

5. Fold the napkin in half so the front is supported by the folds in the back, or fold it into thirds, tucking the ends into each other for additional support.

Banded Beauty

This fold is lovely on its own, but it can be enhanced even further by tucking something into one of the folds. This could be a sprig of rosemary, a small flower, a name tag — or whatever inspires you at the moment.

INSTRUCTIONS:

1. Fold a large (20-inch is best) napkin into quarters.

2. Working with the loose corners in the upper right, roll down the top layer so that it lies just past the center of the napkin.

3. Take the next layer and roll it down, tucking it under the first layer.

4. With the third layer, roll the material under instead of over so that it goes in the opposite direction of the other rolls. It will stay tucked in this way.

5. Next, fold the right and left sides of the napkin under so that it is in thirds, with the center one-third facing up and displaying the bands.

6. Place the napkin on the table as is, or tuck something into one of the bands.

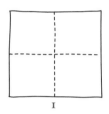

I

2

3

4

5

Pine Cone

The multi-layered look of this napkin will have your guests thinking you are a napkin-folding whiz. In fact, putting it together is easier than you think!

INSTRUCTIONS:

1. Working with a large, square napkin, bring up the bottom-right corner to within a couple of inches of the opposite corner.

2. Turn the napkin so that you are working with a large triangle, flat side down, and then turn it over.

3. Fold up the right and left sides so that the bottom edges are perpendicular to the bottom edge. There should be an inch or two of space between the folded edges in the center.

4. Next, fold up the bottom edge about an inch or so.

5. Turn the napkin over again, and bring the right and left sides in so the napkin is folded into thirds.

6. Tuck the left side into the right side, stand the napkin up, and puff it out with your hand.

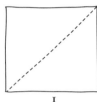

1

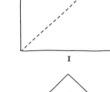

2

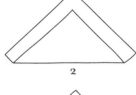

3

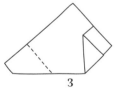

4

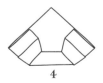

5

6

Four-Leaf Clover

This is a wonderful napkin to use for a
St. Patrick's Day dinner — especially if you
have large green napkins — but it's appropriate
for any time you could use a little luck in your life.

INSTRUCTIONS:

1. With a large, square napkin, fold each of its corners so they meet in the center.

2. Fold the corners in again so they also meet in the center.

3. Turn the napkin over, and fold the corners over again to meet in the center.

4. Place a glass in the center of the napkin to secure it while you work your way around the fold, and pull out each of the corners from underneath. You may want to do this where you will position the napkin on the table so you don't have to pick it up and move it once it's fluffed.

5. Gently pull up on each corner so it sits up properly.

1

2

3

4

5

Cock's Comb

Using a bright-red napkin for this fold will give it the flair it deserves. Use a large napkin for this one, and be sure the material is neither too thick nor too flimsy. It needs to be solid enough so that the edges will stay up, but not so heavy that it looks too bulky.

INSTRUCTIONS:

I. Fold the square napkin into quarters.

2. With the loose corners facing down, fold the napkin diagonally to form a triangle with the loose corners at the top.

3. Holding the triangle at the top, bring in both the right and left sides of the napkin so the edges are in the center.

4. Fold the lower points up and under the napkin.

5. Next, fold the triangle in half, bringing the left side under the right side. This will cause the center to open slightly.

6. Lay the napkin down so that the corner points are facing up. Then, while holding the base, begin to gently pull up each of the corners to form the cock's comb.

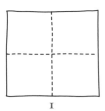

I

2

3

4

5

6

Butterfly

A wonderful fold for a fancy luncheon!

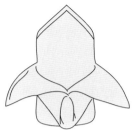

INSTRUCTIONS:

1. Fold a large, square napkin in half diagonally to form an equal-sided triangle.

2. Place the bottom fold along the bottom.

3. Bring up the right and left corners so the edges meet in the center and the tips at the top corner. This will create a point facing down.

4. Bring up the bottom point to within an inch or so of the top point.

5. Lower the point of the bottom fold so that it touches the bottom edge of the napkin.

6. Turn the napkin over, and bring in both the left and right sides toward the center, tucking one end into the other.

7. Stand the napkin up, and, holding it securely, pull down the left and right sides to create the butterfly's "wings."

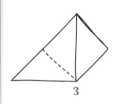

Candle

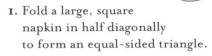

Elegant and stately on their own, napkins folded into this shape can also be grouped for a buffet. When done this way, they look like a lineup of soldiers.

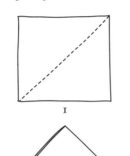

1

INSTRUCTIONS:

1. Fold a large, square napkin in half diagonally to form an equal-sided triangle.

2. Place the bottom fold along the bottom.

3. Bring up the bottom edge an inch or two.

4. Turn the napkin over and roll it up so it is fairly tight and compact.

5. Stand the napkin up and tuck the exposed corner into the cuff of the fold to hold it in place. For an added candle effect, fold down a layer at the top to resemble dripped wax.

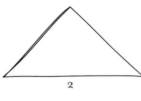

2

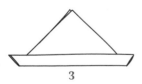

3

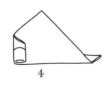

4

5

Home Sweet Home

When folded, this napkin looks like a child's drawing of a house, complete with a square background. This fold could show off your monogram, but you'd have to work it in upside down. With its clean, flat surface, it is also the perfect size and shape for a namecard or a party token.

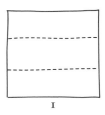

INSTRUCTIONS:

1. Fold a large square napkin into thirds, and position it so the fold is at the top.

2. Putting your finger on the top fold in the center of the napkin, fold down the right side.

3. Next, take the corner of the napkin that now extends beyond the rectangle, and fold it up so that the end of the napkin forms a tight triangle.

4. Finally, fold the napkin in half, working from right to left so that the house shape sits on the square.

Fleur-de-Lis

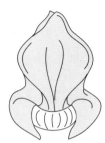

This napkin fold is designed to look like the centuries-old emblem of the fleur-de-lis, which has its roots in ancient heraldry. In French, lis means lily, and the symbol is a stylized representation of this lovely flower, with a high point and two sides. It has become synonymous with French royalty and will give your table the royal treatment wherever it is placed.

INSTRUCTIONS:

1. Fold a large, square napkin in half diagonally to form a triangle.

2. Position the napkin so that the folded edge is at the bottom, and bring up about one-third of the napkin so that it's folded over to resemble a paper hat.

3. Turn the napkin over, and working from left to right, fold the napkin into one-inch-wide accordion folds.

4. Put the bottom of the napkin into a napkin ring (perhaps one with a crown motif?), and gently pull the sides until you have the desired fleur-de-lis configuration.

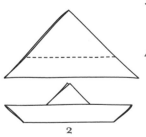

2

3

4

Paper Vase

This crisp, simple fold creates a pocket into which you can slip a single stem of your favorite flower — the perfect luncheon pick-me-up!

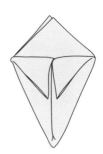

INSTRUCTIONS:

1. Fold a large, square napkin in half diagonally to form a triangle.

2. Position the napkin so the folded edge is at the bottom.

3. Fold the two outer corners into the center so their edges meet and the corner points are aligned at the top of the napkin.

4. Starting on the right side, fold the new corner in toward the center so that its edge runs along the centerline.

5. Repeat Step 4 on the left side.

6. Finally, fold over the corners that have formed the straight line below the pointed top of the napkin so the pouch is revealed, and tuck in your flower.

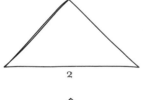

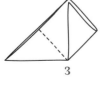

Amaryllis

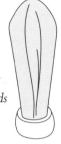

This elongated fold is best done with a sturdy or starched napkin so that it remains standing once completed. The base into which you place it must be sturdy as well, so use a heavily weighted napkin ring or another heavy decorative item that you can place it in. Its statuesque nature lends it to a central location for the diner, typically the center of the plate.

INSTRUCTIONS:

1. Fold a large, square napkin in half diagonally to form a triangle.

2. Position the napkin so the folded edge is at the bottom.

3. Fold the two outer corners into the center so their edges meet and the corner points are aligned at the top of the napkin.

4. Turn the napkin over. It will look like a diamond. Bring in the right- and left-hand corners so that the points meet in the center.

5. Next, fold down the top point so that it, too, meets the other points in the center.

6. Turn the napkin upside down so the point is facing up, and fold in both the left and right sides so the edges meet in the center.

7. Turn the napkin over, and position it in the napkin ring.

1

2

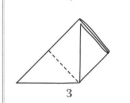

3

4

5

6

Blossom

The best way to show off the blossom fold is to place it into a glass. This way, diners can see the folds that create its base, it won't fall over, and you can really bring out the blossom element of the fold. A short, squat glass is best.

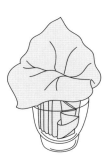

INSTRUCTIONS:

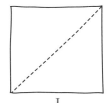

I

1. Fold a large, square napkin in half diagonally to form a triangle.

2. Position the napkin so the folded edge is at the bottom.

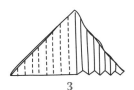

3

3. Working from one corner to the next, fold the napkin into accordion pleats about one inch wide. Crease the folds so they stay firm.

4

4. Put the napkin into the glass with the top point facing up, and gently fluff out the two sides to form the blossom.

Birthday Hat

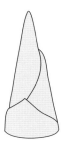

Putting this fold together with a selection of brightly colored napkins placed on a crisp, white tablecloth will make the table look like a giant birthday cake. Add balloons and some confetti, and you have a very festive table!

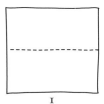

I

INSTRUCTIONS:

1. Fold a large, square napkin in half to form a rectangle.

2. Position the napkin so the folded edge is at the top.

3. Fold down the top-right corner so that the point meets the bottom edge.

3

4. From the left corner, begin to roll the napkin in toward the center so that it forms a cone shape.

4

5. When the cone is vertical and near the center, take the right side of the napkin and fold it around the cone.

5

6. Bring up the point that faces down so that it covers and secures the bottom-right fold.

7. Turn it over and stand it up.

6

7

The Winner

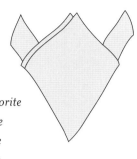

This is a great fold to use if you or your family are celebrating a victory of some kind — a raise or promotion, a championship game, or even your favorite sports team's success. The finished fold will make the letter "W" — so put it flat on top of the dinner plate for the full effect. If you're celebrating a sports team, you can use a napkin in the team's color.

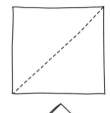

1

INSTRUCTIONS

1. Working from a large, square napkin, fold it into a triangle so the fold is along the bottom edge.

2. Take the bottom edge and bring it up a couple of inches so you have what looks like a paper hat.

3. With your finger at the center on the bottom fold, bring the right side over so the point sticks up.

4. Now bring the left side over so its point forms the other part of the "W."

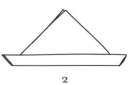

2

3

4

Surprise Package

This tidy fold is deceptive, thus its name. From the top, it looks like a simple design. Take it out of its napkin ring, though, and it reveals multiple layers.

INSTRUCTIONS:

1. Fold a large, square napkin into quarters, and position it so the free corners are at the top and the folded corner is at the bottom.

2. Working from the left or right, begin to fold the napkin into accordion pleats of about one inch wide.

3. Slide the napkin into a napkin ring so that the ring is in the center, and bunch it out a bit at the top and bottom.

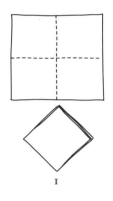

1

2

3

Peacock

The idea behind this fold is to shape it so that one end looks like the long, languorous tail-feathers of a peacock. This is done by putting the fold into a wine glass. The body sits in the cup of the glass, and the "tail" stretches down the stem to the table.

INSTRUCTIONS:

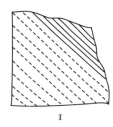

1. Using a large, square napkin, start at the bottom-left or upper-right corner and begin folding the entire napkin into one-inch accordion pleats.

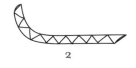

2. Laying the pleated napkin down horizontally, bring up the left side so that it is curving up like a neck, about three inches above the body.

3. Position the bottom curve of the neck in the wine glass so the short and long ends stick out from either side.

4. Gently fluff out the folds to form the peacock.

Together Forever

The way that this fold joins both sides of the napkin and also bands it together is symbolic of a perfect union. When placed to the side of the fork, it makes for a classic arrangement, too.

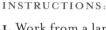

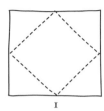

INSTRUCTIONS:

I. Work from a large, square napkin in a square position.

2. Bring in each of the corners so the tips meet in the middle.

3. Fold the napkin in half to form a rectangle, and then fold it in half again to form a small square.

4. Starting in the top-right corner, roll the first layer of napkin in and under so that it forms a band.

5. Roll the second corner under in the opposite direction.

6. Turn the napkin so that the bands are faced horizontally instead of on an angle.

7. Finish the fold by bringing in the corners and folding them under the napkin.

Fountain

The upward cascade of this fold is reminiscent of a shooting fountain — and the effect is accented when you use an edged napkin. Placing it in a napkin ring so that it stands up lends additional grandeur.

INSTRUCTIONS:

1. Fold a large, square napkin into quarters.

2. Working with the free corners at the bottom, fold up the first layer so the point meets the point at the top.

3. Bring up and fold the next layer so that the point is about an inch below the top.

4. Continue bringing up the layers and folding them so that they are within an inch or so of each other.

5. Turn the napkin over, and fold the right side diagonally over the center. Repeat with the left side.

6. Finally, fold up the point at the bottom of the napkin, turn it over to display the fountain, and place the bottom in a strong napkin ring.

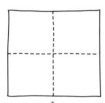

1

2

3

4

5

6

Poinsettia

Use a large red napkin for this fold, and show it off at Christmas time.

INSTRUCTIONS:

1. Fold in each corner of the napkin so that the tips meet in the center.

2. Turn the napkin over, and fold over the bottom-left and top-right corners so that their tips meet in the center.

3. Position the napkin horizontally with the folded corners at the top and bottom, and then fold the napkin in half, bringing the top over the bottom.

4. Working from the left or the right, fold the napkin into one-inch-wide accordion pleats from one end to the other.

5. Place the short end of the napkin into a wine glass. Gently pull out and down on the left and right sides to create a rounded top.

6. Form the front petals by gently pulling down on the front corners. Fluff so that it looks like a poinsettia bloom.

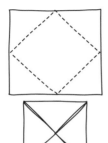

1

2

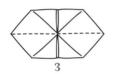

3

4

5

Pirate's Hat

*You can treat this fold playfully and keep it
as a pirate's hat, or you can accentuate its
pyramid look for a more formal statement.
Place the napkin with the tip facing up,
or position it so that the tip points left.*

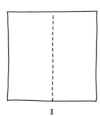

1

INSTRUCTIONS:

1. Fold a large, square napkin in half from
   right to left to form a vertical rectangle,
   with the folded edge to the right.

2. With your finger marking the center,
   fold in the upper-right corner so that it
   crosses just over the center of the napkin.
   Do the same thing on the left side.

3. Turning the napkin over, fold in the
   bottom-right and -left corners as you
   did with the top corners.

4. Fold the bottom part of the napkin up
   so its top is about an inch away from the
   very top.

5. Finally, fold about two inches of the
   napkin up from the bottom to create the
   final flap.

2

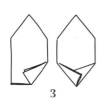

3

4

Water Lily

This is another fold that should be propped in a glass to look its best. When it is, you'll see that it is really beautiful.

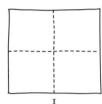

INSTRUCTIONS:

1. Fold a large, square napkin into quarters.

2. Position the folded napkin so that the loose ends are at the top and the folded edge is at the bottom.

3. Fold up the bottom corner about three inches, and fold the napkin in half from left to right.

4. Working from the right, fold one-inch-wide accordion pleats until you reach the center.

5. Repeat Step 4 from the left side.

6. Place the bottom of the napkin into a glass, and fluff out the top to give it a graceful appearance.

Wiesbaden

This is a traditional fold from Germany;
it originated in the town of Wiesbaden.
For this one, you'll want to work with a
smaller square napkin — about 17 inches
square. You'll love the results.

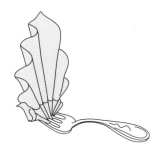

INSTRUCTIONS:

1. Fold a square napkin in half diagonally to form a triangle.

2. Position the napkin so that the folded edge is at the bottom.

3. Bring up the bottom edge about an inch and a half, and crease the fold.

4. Working from right to left, fold the napkin into one-inch-wide accordion pleats until you get to the end.

5. Position the pleats between the tines of a fork.

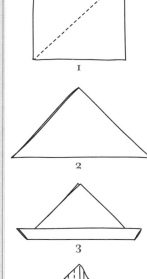

Four Feathers

A fun fold for the Thanksgiving table — or any time you want a plumed look.

INSTRUCTIONS:

1. Fold a large, square napkin in half diagonally to form a triangle.

2. Position the napkin so that the folded edge is at the bottom.

3. Bring the right corner over and across the far edge of the left side so that the point is going beyond the left corner.

4. Repeat Step 3 twice more so that there are four points on the left side of the napkin.

5. Fold the remaining top point under the napkin so that the "feathers" face front.

6. Position the napkin in a glass.

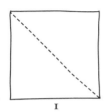

1

2

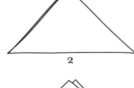

3

4

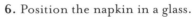

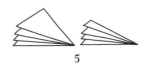

5   6

Simple Sailboat

Your seafaring friends and family will get a kick out of this one!

INSTRUCTIONS:

1. Fold a large, square napkin in half diagonally to form a triangle.

2. Position the napkin so that the folded edge is at the bottom.

3. Bring the right corner over to the left corner to form another triangle.

4. Reposition the napkin so that the longest edge is at the bottom.

5. Bring in the right and left sides so their edges meet in the center, as if you were making a paper airplane.

6. Fold up the right corner so that it is even with the bottom of the triangle. Tuck it behind the top layer, and repeat with the left side.

7. Craft a hull of sorts by rolling up the bottom edge around the front and back "sails" of the triangle.

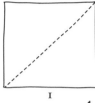

1

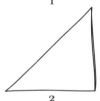

2

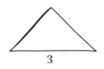

3

4

5

6

7

Invitation

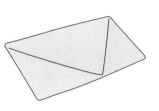

What better way for guests to feel like they're part of the "in" crowd at your house than with a fold that resembles an envelope? Put a special note inside if you want to make it even more special.

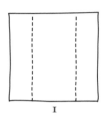

INSTRUCTIONS:

1. Working with a large, square napkin, bring the left and right sides in so that their edges meet in the center and form a vertical rectangle.

2. Fold the bottom edge up so that it reaches the center, and repeat with the top part of the napkin so its edge meets in the center.

3. Working on the top part of the napkin, fold in the right and left corners to form a triangle on top of a rectangle.

4. Fold the triangular top over the bottom to complete the Invitation.

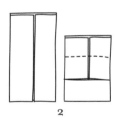

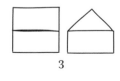

Rollin'

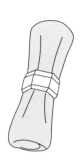

Why is something that is so simple to construct included with the Impressive Folds? Because there are so many ways you can dress this one up! The band you put in the middle can be anything from snazzy (monogrammed napkin rings or paper) to silly (teething rings, if you're having a baby shower). This is a great buffet fold, too, because you can put the cutlery inside the napkin before you roll it up, if you want.

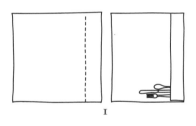

INSTRUCTIONS:

1. Working with a large, square napkin, bring in and tightly fold about three inches of the material from the right side. If you want to add silverware, position it inside the fold.

2. Bring the left side of the napkin over so that the edge meets the far edge.

3. Turn the napkin over and, working from the bottom, roll it up toward the top.

4. For a very neat appearance, leave about two inches at the top, fold half of that in so there is a nice clean line, and complete the roll.

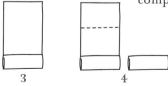

Rose

*To provide the ultimate in elegance with this fold,
try to coordinate the color of the napkin you use
with the color of the roses you have on the table or
in the room. Reds, pinks, yellows, whites — all are beautiful.*

INSTRUCTIONS:

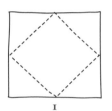

1. Working with a large, square napkin, fold all four corners in so their tips meet in the center and the napkin forms a diamond.

2. Bring the corners in again to form a square.

3. Keeping careful hold of the napkin, turn it over, and then fold the corners in again to form a square.

4. Place the base of a glass in the center of the fold to secure the napkin while you tug the corners from underneath to fluff them into petals.

5. Remove the glass, and carefully turn the napkin over.

6. Pull out a point from each side on the front, and then fluff the innermost points to create the center petals.

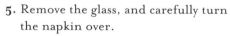

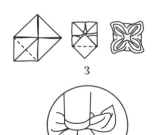

Hydrangea

This fold resembles not the multi-petaled rose, but the big and puffy hydrangea. Like the fold for the rose, though, when done with a napkin whose color matches a bouquet of flowers, or perhaps a pattern on the tablecloth, it's truly stunning.

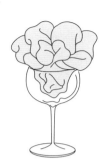

INSTRUCTIONS:

1. Fold a large, square napkin into quarters.

2. Position it so that the loose ends are facing the top.

3. Bring the bottom edge up about an inch, and then fold the right side over the left so the points meet.

4. Doing the right side first, fold from the outside tip to the longer edge in accordion pleats.

5. Repeat Step 4 on the left side.

6. Put the napkin in a glass, and create the hydrangea by fluffing out the four layers.

7. Tuck in the corner points to complete the look.

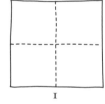

2

3

4

6

7

Court Jester

*If you like a fold with a whimsical side,
this one is for you.*

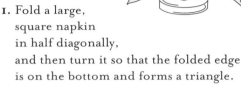

INSTRUCTIONS:

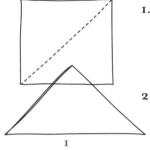

1

1. Fold a large,
   square napkin
   in half diagonally,
   and then turn it so that the folded edge
   is on the bottom and forms a triangle.

2. Placing your finger in the center of the
   bottom edge, bring up both the right
   and left sides so their edges form a "V"
   at the bottom of the napkin.

3. Fold up the bottom about three or four
   inches so that it forms a smaller triangle.

4. Next, fold down the top of that triangle
   so its point meets the bottom edge.

5. Working from one side to the next, fold
   the entire napkin into accordion pleats.

6. Put the bottom of the napkin in a glass,
   but be sure to keep the small triangle in
   front outside of the glass.

7. Gently tug the sides to form wings.

2

3

4

5

6

Classic Tulip

This makes a lovely, soft fold that is as beautiful as a Georgia O'Keeffe painting.

INSTRUCTIONS:

1. Starting with a large, square napkin, fold it into thirds to form a horizontal rectangle (the folded edge should be on the top).

2. Bring in both the left and right sides so their edges meet in the center.

3. Starting on the right, bring the pointed corner up so that its side is parallel to the center. Repeat with the left side.

4. Turn the napkin over, and bring the upper right corner over and slightly across the center. Do the same with the left side, tucking the ends together.

5. Turn the napkin over and stand it up.

6. Gently pull at the sides to create the tulip's petals.

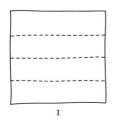

1

2

3

4

5

6

Double Fan

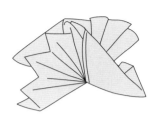

If the regular fan-fold is becoming too routine in your household, you can shake things up with this more elaborate double-sided fan. It looks great placed in the center of the plate.

INSTRUCTIONS:

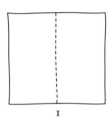

1. Fold a large, square napkin in half vertically to form a rectangle, with the folded edge on the left.

2. Starting at the bottom, make one-inch accordion pleats until you have gone one pleat beyond the center of the napkin.

3. Turn the napkin over, and take the upper-left corner down so that its point meets the bottom edge, forming a triangle over the pleats.

4. Fold the right side over to the left side.

5. Bring the top left edge down and over the pleats, and then fold up the bottom-left edge so that it lies along the bottom side of the pleats.

6. Stand the napkin up by opening the pleats on either side.

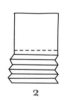

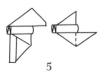

Fortune Cookie

Another fun shape to play with if you like putting notes in your napkins.

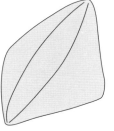

INSTRUCTIONS:

1. Working with a large, square napkin, fold the bottom up one-third and the top down one-third so that you have formed a horizontal rectangle.

2. With your finger in the center as a guide, fold down the right and then the left corners so their edges meet in the center. There will be about an inch or so of overlap on the bottom.

3. Fold the rectangular overlaps into triangles by bringing their corners up.

4. Fold the left side of the napkin over the right side so the bottom edge meets the top, and do the same thing on the right side, forming a square.

5. Position the napkin into a diamond shape, and fold it in half.

6. Prop the napkin on the plate so that the bottom slit becomes the front of the napkin. This is where you put your "fortune."

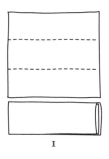

1

3

4

5

6

Monarch Butterfly

*Brightly colored napkins folded into this
butterfly pattern will transform your table
into a summertime meadow.*

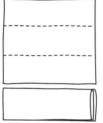

I

2

3

4

INSTRUCTIONS:

1. Fold a large, square
napkin in thirds, bringing the top fold
down first so that the bottom fold comes
up and over it to form a horizontal
rectangle.

2. Fold in the left side about one-third of
the way, and then fold that back on itself
so its edge is now flush with the outside
edge.

3. Repeat Step 2 on the right side of the
napkin.

4. On each side, lift the top layers and tuck
their corners under to form "wings."

Napkin Wrapper

This is a wonderful touch for a birthday party, Christmas dinner, or any occasion at which you want to give a small gift. It holds only a small, cube-like box, suitable for a gift such as a small ornament, jewelry, or gourmet chocolate. Fold these on an ironing board so you can secure your pleats.

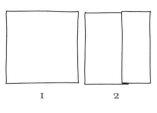

1

2

3

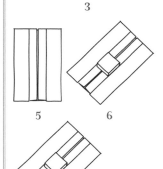

5   6

7   9

INSTRUCTIONS:

1. Using a large, square napkin, position the box in the center, and form a crease with your fingers along both long sides.

2. Bring the sides of the napkin up, and firmly crease along these lines to create a pleat in the middle of the napkin.

3. Create a second pleat parallel to and on top of the first pleat, and about a half-inch from the folded edge of the first pleat.

4. Go over all of these with an iron.

5. Repeat, making a third pleat on top of the second one.

6. Turn the napkin over, and position it like a diamond. Place the box in the center of the napkin.

7. Fold up the bottom corner about an inch, flattening the edge. Do the same for the top corner.

8. Bring the flat-edged sides up over the box.

9. Bring the right and left sides of the napkin up, and tie with string or ribbon.

About Cider Mill Press Book Publishers

Good ideas ripen with time. From seed to harvest, Cider Mill Press strives to bring fine reading, information, and entertainment together between the covers of its creatively crafted books. Our Cider Mill bears fruit twice a year, publishing a new crop of titles each spring and fall.

Visit us on the Web at
www.cidermillpress.com
or write to us at
12 Port Farm Road
Kennebunkport, Maine 04046